THE TRUTH IS

1. Leveling up your craft to write a story that lives long after you've left the planet is what some might call a ridiculous goal.

2. You will not tell that story after reading just one how-to-write book.

3. You will not tell that story as the result of taking one seminar.

4. You know creating a timeless work of art will require the dedication of a world-class athlete. You will be training your mind with as much ferocity and single-minded purpose as an Olympic gold medal hopeful. That kind of cognitive regimen excites you, but you just haven't found a convincing storytelling dojo to do that work.

5. The path to leveling up your creative craft is a dark and treacherous one. You've been at it a long time, and it often feels like you're wearing three-dimensional horse blinders. More times than you'd like to admit, you're not sure if you're moving north or south or east or west. And the worst part? You can't see anyone else, anywhere, going through what you're going through. You're all alone.

WELCOME TO THE STORY GRID UNIVERSE

HERE'S HOW WE CONTEND WITH THOSE TRUTHS

1. We believe we find meaning in the pursuit of creations that last longer than we do. This is *not* ridiculous. Seizing opportunities and overcoming obstacles as we stretch ourselves to reach for seemingly unreachable creations is transformational. We believe this pursuit is the most valuable and honorable way to spend our time here. Even if—especially if—we never reach our lofty creative goals.

2. Writing just one story isn't going to take us to the top. We're moving from point A to Point A^{5000}. We've got lots of mountains to climb, lots of rivers and oceans to cross, and many deep dark forests to traverse along the way. We need topographic guides, and if they're not available, we'll have to figure out how to write them ourselves.

3. We're drawn to seminars to consume the imparted wisdom of an icon in the arena, but we leave with something far more valuable than the curriculum. We get to meet the universe's other pilgrims and compare notes on the terrain.

4. The Story Grid Universe has a virtual dojo, a university in which to work out and get stronger—a place to stumble, correct mistakes, and stumble again, until the moves become automatic and mesmerizing to outside observers.

5. The Story Grid Universe has a performance space, a publishing house dedicated to leveling up the craft with clear boundaries of progress and the ancillary reference resources to pack for each project mission. There are an infinite number of paths to where you want to be, with a story that works. Seeing how others have made it down their own yellow-brick roads to release their creations into the timeless creative cosmos will help keep you on the straight and narrow path.

All are welcome—the more, the merrier. But please abide by the golden rule:

Put the work above all else, and trust the process.

THE WRITERS' COMMON LANGUAGE

A SHARED VOCABULARY TO TELL BETTER STORIES

TIM GRAHL

STORY GRID

STORY GRID

Story Grid Publishing LLC
223 Egremont Plain Road
PMB 191
Egremont, MA 01230

Copyright (c) 2021 Story Grid Publishing LLC
Cover Design by Magnus Rex
Edited by Leslie Watts

All Rights Reserved

First Story Grid Publishing Paperback Edition
February 2021

For Information about Special Discounts for Bulk Purchases,
Please visit www.storygridpublishing.com

ISBN: 978-1-64501-064-7
Ebook: 978-1-64501-065-4

For

All Past, Present, and Future Story Nerds

INTRODUCTION

It was the summer of 2015 and I had finally made the decision.

I was going to take this writing thing seriously.

For years I had been writing in fits and starts. I had even self-published a couple of nonfiction business titles. However, I really wanted to write fiction.

I have always been a big reader. I grew up in a religious home where television, movies and music were strictly controlled. Somehow, though, books fell through the cracks of the rules. I think my parents assumed reading was a good habit, so how much trouble could I really get into?

My mom would take me to the bookstore (she was terrified of libraries, but that's another story) and let me buy any books I wanted. I would take them home and devour them.

As a child, my favorite author was Michael Crichton. I still remember reading *Jurassic Park* and being terrified. I had nightmares about velociraptors chasing me, but I never told my parents because I was afraid they would figure out I shouldn't be reading this stuff.

I burned through all of Crichton's and Grisham's titles and read whatever else I could get my hands on. I loved escaping into these grown-up thrilling worlds where life and death were constantly at stake!

This reading habit followed me into adulthood, but along the way I had a dream of writing my own stories. I wanted to tell ones that made people feel the way I felt when I read.

So I began writing. I would start working on something, get a little way in, realize it was rubbish, and stop working. A couple times I won NaNoWriMo—National Novel Writing Month where writers from all over the world attempt to finish a fifty-thousand-word novel during the month of November—but, when I read my novel, I could see it was poorly written.

However, during the summer of 2015, I decided it would be different this time. I had to start writing fiction again. And not just put words down but figuring out how to tell a great story.

As I tend to do before embarking on any new project, I started reading books. I read *Save the Cat* by Blake Snyder and *Story* by Robert McKee. I reread *On Writing* by Stephen King and *Bird by Bird* by Anne Lamott. I burned through *On Writing Well* by William Zinsser and Strunk and White's *The Elements of Style*. There were plenty of others, but you get the idea.

These all helped, but they were missing something. I knew on some level there had to be an underlying order to storytelling. I wanted to learn the structure of story. I needed to know why the stories I wrote didn't work and how to fix them.

This is when I finally picked up *The Story Grid* by Shawn Coyne. I bought it as soon it came out, but it went on my shelf right away. At eight and a half by eleven inches, 344 pages, and almost two pounds of dead trees, it was quite the intimidating read.

But after reading my way through the other options and not finding what I needed, I finally gave *The Story Grid* a try.

I wasn't far into it before bells started going off in my head.

This was what I had been looking for!

I read it cover to cover, understanding only portions of it. I read it again, underlining and highlighting sections.

I didn't know it then, but what I was seeking was a common language that allowed me to think clearly and have intelligent conversations about story.

Every time I tried to talk to other writers and editors, it was as if I was in another country that spoke an unfamiliar language and was asking for directions. I would point and gesticulate and talk much louder than necessary, and they would listen carefully before pointing and talking without either of us making any progress.

Reading *The Story Grid* was the first time I encountered real, concrete words with clear definitions applied to this creative process of writing.

Through a happy coincidence, Shawn and I met through my business, so I reached out to him to see if we could talk for a few minutes. He obliged. That phone call turned into a weekly podcast where he coached me through the art of storytelling.

I have a confession. At this point in my journey, I did not understand what editors do. I thought they were the people who fixed your misplaced commas and misspelled words. They might also clean up your sentence structure along the way.

This, of course, is important work. It has to be done, but only at the end when the story works. I knew that cleaning up my grammar wasn't enough to fix my books.

After working with Shawn, I realized that editing was *much* more than grammatical mastery.

The first thing a good editor does is provide a common language and toolbox.

Why is this so important?

If you ask ten different writers to explain what the word "genre" means, you will probably get ten different answers. You will also get divergent answers in discussions about acts, sequences, scene types, characterization, and other common words and phrases.

Before we can have a real discussion or even think about fixing our stories, we must understand the meaning of the words we are using. When my editor says, "inciting incident," it's helpful to know that what *I* think an inciting incident is and what *she* thinks an inciting incident is are the same thing.

Until we have a shared language, we cannot have a real discussion about our writing.

The second thing a good editor brings to the table is the ability and perspective to provide clear, concrete feedback.

If you have ever tried to get feedback on your writing from other writers, it can be maddening. Here's an example I've used before.

"That character isn't really believable."

"The dialogue is a little 'meh.'"

"It's too long."

"It's too short."

"You need to fix the ending."

While these things may be true, they aren't clear, solvable problems. How do you fix dialogue that is "meh"?

Imagine if you had the same conversation with a car mechanic:

Me: "Did you take a look at my car?"

Mechanic: "Yeah, something is wrong with it."

Me: "Yeah ... I kind of thought that, but I wasn't sure. What's wrong with it?"

Mechanic: "Your engine isn't running right."

Me: "Okay, what's wrong with it?"

Mechanic: "It's running a little soft."

Me: "Okay ... what does that mean?"

Mechanic: "It's just not working for me."

Me: "Which part? What needs to be fixed?"

Mechanic: "I don't know. You just need to work on it."

Me: [falls to knees sobbing]

A good editor doesn't offer fuzzy, vague feedback. They identify concrete, clear problems that are fixable.

The goal of this book is to share some foundational language and tools that Story Grid provides to help us think clearly about and discuss our stories. This will increase our ability to:

1. Edit our own work. We're often told that we're too close to our own writing to edit it properly. While it's true that we need an editor toward the end of our project, once we become familiar with the Story Grid toolbox, we can create much better stories on our own.

2. Work with our editor. With a shared language and toolbox along with the ability to identify problems, working with our editor will become much easier and more efficient.

Let's get started.

1
GENRE

Have you ever played that desert island game? There are different iterations, but you always have to pick a certain number of your favorite books/movies/songs that you would take with you if you were stranded alone on an island.

So let's play together. Pick your five favorite books you would take with you if you were stranded on a desert island.

Got them?

Okay, now take away two of them. Which three would you keep?

You know what's coming. Right?

Take away two more.

What is the one book you can't live without?

It's hard to choose just one.

This is the same problem most of us run into when it's time to pick the story we are going to tell.

When I first started working with Shawn, I had so many ideas for the story I wanted to write. I wanted to tell a story with elements of crime and romance and war. I wanted big sweeping tales with a vast cast of characters.

While some stories have all these things, you must pick one of these ideas that is the true focus of your story.

On my first call with Shawn, I started talking about all the things I wanted to write about. However, when I turned in a scene for him to read, it became clear I didn't understand what the story was about or where I was going with it.

This is when Shawn introduced me to an accurate definition of *genre*.

If we ask most writers about genre—me included at the time—they might say things like fantasy, romance, mystery, steampunk, thriller, etc.

But what does any of this actually mean?

If someone tells us they're writing a fantasy story, what do we know about the *story*? We might get an idea of the setting, but we know nothing about what is happening in the story. What problems do the characters face? What do they want or need? Saying we are writing a fantasy story doesn't answer these questions because "fantasy" isn't what the story is about.

Inside of Story Grid, genre has a specific meaning.

There are twelve content genres. They are either external—Action, Horror, Crime, Western/Eastern, War, Thriller, Society, Love, or Performance—or internal—Worldview, Morality, or Status. When we dig a little deeper, we notice the word genre is merely shorthand for something else.

When an editor asks what genre you are writing in, they want to know what your story is *about*. What is the value of the story? What is the most important thing in your story? What kind of change happens in your story? Where are the characters at the beginning versus the end of your story?

Here's the kicker, like the desert island game, you can only pick one for your story.

Yes, our story can have elements of many genres, but one value should drive the story. Just like we can go on a road trip with a bunch of friends, but we shouldn't all have a hand on the steering wheel at the same time.

Often during our calls, Shawn would let me ramble on and on, talking about all the different things I wanted to write about, but he would eventually bring me back to this question.

What is your story about?

What is the value at stake for the protagonist?

Is our protagonist's life being threatened at every turn? We are writing in the Action genre. Is our protagonist going to find love? We are writing a Love story.

This is the first thing our editor should talk to us about. Without knowing our genre, we don't know and will find it hard to explain what our story is about.

We'll have no idea from scene to scene if we are on the right track. Our line-by-line prose could be masterful and beautiful, but ultimately the story will fall flat.

Early on when I struggled to understand genre, Shawn introduced me to Maslow's Hierarchy of Needs. Abraham Maslow developed this model to understand human motivation.

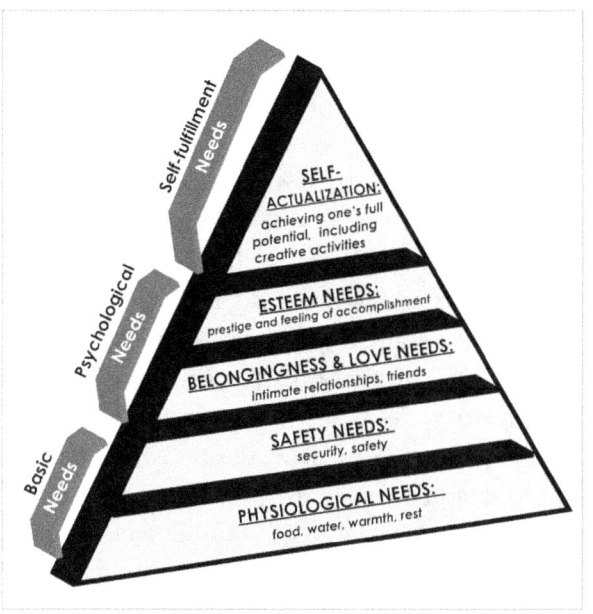

In real life, we focus on one of these layers at a time. If we don't have enough food or water, that becomes our number one concern above all else. But once we meet our physiological and safety needs, we have the mental space to focus on our friends and closest relationships, and so on.

We can map the Story Grid content genres on this hierarchy of basic human needs as well. For example, the Action genre deals with life and death and therefore focuses on physiological needs. Love deals with love and hate and focuses on the need for belonging and love. Performance is focused on our need for esteem.

Makes sense, right?

When we choose our genre, we are identifying what our protagonist needs in their life throughout our story. This is what our character values the most. If they are stranded on a desert island with no food or water, it's clear both what the problem is and when they solve it. Our protagonist dies or lives. That's an Action story.

As we move up the hierarchy, the genres become squishier, and we move toward the internal genres that deal with internal conflict. In a Worldview story we're now talking about self-actualization and the end goal is more subtle.

Another way to think about genre is to ask the question, what does our protagonist want and need throughout the story? We call this the Object of Desire. Toward the bottom of Maslow's pyramid, our story is about our character's conscious want—survival or safety. As we move up the pyramid, it becomes more about our character's unconscious need.

However, in all these areas, we focus on one need. One value.

One genre.

Choosing a genre keeps us from getting off track while we write. Our genre becomes our beacon, always pointing us in the right direction.

Genre also makes it easier to have a conversation about our story. Instead of a loose idea of "is this working?" we can have a discussion with our editor around the value at stake in our story.

This makes a *huge* difference.

Even if our scene is beautifully written, if it doesn't fit in our genre, it doesn't fit in our story.

Genre is the first word in our new story language and toolbox. It's the first tool we come back to over and over.

What is the genre? What need is most important to our protagonist?

Genre is important, but it is macro. It's the high-level view of our story. Next we must dive into what we need in our story to make sure it meets reader expectations for our genre.

2
CONVENTIONS AND OBLIGATORY MOMENTS

This past weekend my wife and I watched the movie *Holidate*. It's the holiday season as I write this, and Netflix has released this as a new Love story. I wondered if it would meet the expectations for that genre. Sure enough, about three-fourths of the way through the movie, the two lovers break up and it looks like they are done for good. Gasp! This is the "lovers break up" moment.

Same thing with the latest *Mission: Impossible* movie I watched with my kids. Toward the end of the story, there's a moment when our hero, Ethan Hunt, has tried everything and nothing has worked. The villain, August Walker, is about to win. This is the "hero at the mercy of the villain" moment.

These, of course, are not spoilers. They are moments in the story that must happen for us to be satisfied as consumers of the story.

You see this in every great story. The "lovers meet" at the beginning of a Love story. The giant, final battle in a War story. The big, everything-rides-on-this concert at the end of a Performance story. The showdown with the monster in a Horror story.

What are these things? Why are they in every story? Inside of Story Grid, we call these obligatory moments.

However, these obligatory moments don't just happen. They are set up by conventions that are particular to our genre. Every Crime story needs someone trying to solve the crime —a detective, perhaps. A Horror story has to have a monster. An Action story kicks off with an initial attack by the villain, what we call the Shadow Agent. Every Love story needs secrets kept from and by the lovers. In a Society story, an enormous power divide exists between a powerful tyrant and the underrepresented class.

Conventions and obligatory moments are circumstances and specific happenings that the reader expects because of the genre of the story.

If you weren't already scared off by our discussion of genre, you might be running for the hills now that we are talking about "convention(al)" and "obligatory" elements in stories.

When Shawn first introduced me to the idea of conventions and obligatory moments, I got nervous too. It sounded like he was asking me to write to a formula, and I wasn't interested in being *that* kind of a writer. I didn't want my stories to end up being fill-in-the-blank, Mad Libs books full of clichés that had readers rolling their eyes.

But once I started learning about what these things are and how they work, it started making a lot of sense to me.

The metaphor that helps me is that of an automobile.

There are thousands of designs for automobiles. We have categories that are like genres such as sedan, coupe, minivan, truck, etc. Within each of those categories we have huge diversity among features, design, price, and so on.

However, every automobile must meet certain *conventions* and *obligations*.

It has to have wheels, a way to turn it on, seats, steering wheel, lights, windshield, and on and on.

There are conventions (wheels, cup holders, seatbelts) and obligations (how the transmission works in the engine and locating the cup holders within arm's reach). Without the conventional parts, the car would not run, and without the obligatory features, the car may run, but it wouldn't work well for the driver.

This is the same in our story.

Every genre has its conventions and obligatory moments. Our story needs these things in order to *work*. They create the minimally viable version of a story in the genre we have picked. Without them, readers will not enjoy our story. Often, they won't consciously know why, but subconsciously they will know there is a problem with the story.

Once we choose our genre, the next step is to identify the conventions and obligatory moments our story must have to meet reader expectations.

This doesn't create a cliché story. In fact, conventions and obligatory moments point to the extremely important parts of our story that we need to innovate.

They also allow us to be better editors of our own stories and add to the common language toolbox between us and our editors.

It changes the conversation from "there is something missing in your ending" to "you don't have the 'speech in praise of the shadow agent' in your story, and that is an obligatory moment of an Action story."

This is the kind of feedback we can use to fix our stories.

Once we wrap our head around this idea of conventions and obligatory moments, our natural next question might be, "what are the conventions and obligatory moments for *my* genre?"

There are two ways we can go about answering this question.

First, there are a lot of resources on the Story Grid website where we identify the conventions and obligatory moments for each of the genres. You can see a compilation of these resources at storygrid.com/story-language.

Second, we can pick three masterworks in our genre and read each of them. Look for the things that show up in each of the stories.

I like to grab the list of conventions and obligatory moments for my genre and identify them in each of the three masterworks. This exercise helps us see that abiding by the genre requirements doesn't create formulaic, cliché stories. You'll see that each author has the same conventions and obligatory moments but comes up with innovative, interesting ways to include them in the story.

By learning what these are in our genre and identifying them in masterworks of our genre, it will get our creative ideas flowing for how we can include these in our own story.

3
GENRE PART TWO

Now let's talk now about secondary genres.

I had to start by explaining genres and saying we can only pick one—our global genre. And that's absolutely true. We have to have one genre and one value driving all the core conventions and obligatory moments of our story.

But also, if I didn't say that up front, Shawn and every other Story Grid Certified Editor would come to my house with torches and pitchforks because this is the hardest thing to get us free-spirited, my-story-is-a-unique-and-precious-unicorn writers to decide.

However, once we have made that decision, we can talk about our secondary genre.

This is where we can weave another genre into our story to give our reader a fuller, more rounded experience. Our global story may be a Crime story that is turning on justice/injustice or a Worldview story that is turning on naïveté/wisdom. However, we could also give our Crime story a Worldview secondary genre to see our protagonist grow during her pursuit of justice (for example, *The Sweetness at the Bottom of the Pie* by Alan Bradley) or give our Worldview story a Crime secondary genre so our story has more intrigue to increase the narrative drive (for example, *To Kill a Mockingbird* by Harper Lee).

This is not to say our story *must* have a secondary genre. If we read James Bond novels (Action), these are straightforward life-and-death stories. Same for the classic Sherlock Holmes stories (Crime), which are strictly about justice and injustice.

However, if we are telling a War story where our character is also shifting internally from naïve to sophisticated, we are telling a story with a secondary genre of Worldview.

In most cases, we will want to pair an external genre—Action, Horror, Crime, Western/Eastern, War, Thriller, Society, Love, Performance—with an internal genre—Worldview, Morality, Status.

We can have a story such as *The Great Gatsby*, which is a global Worldview genre with a Love secondary genre. We can also have *Pride & Prejudice*, a global Love genre with a secondary Worldview genre.

Just as our global genre has a specific value at stake and conventions and obligatory moments, so does our secondary genre.

By splitting my thinking between global genre and secondary genre, it allows me to understand what is happening with my story at different places.

When I was writing *The Threshing*, a global Action story with a Worldview secondary genre, some moments things were happening externally—moments the life-or-death value was at stake for my character. And other moments things were happening for my character internally. She was having to confront her own internal shortcomings and grow beyond them.

Again, we can approach this conversation through the lens of Objects of Desire. Often our global and secondary genres create competing conscious and unconscious wants and needs inside of our characters.

The protagonist may consciously want to be with the man who is the love of her life (Love), but she also unconsciously needs to shed her naïveté and gain some wisdom in order for that to happen (Worldview).

The old detective consciously wants to figure out who killed the shop owner (Crime) but in order to succeed he unconsciously needs to face his own failure to do the right the thing in the past (Morality).

However—and I can't stress this enough—the major shifts in our story must involve our global genre. Our secondary genre always takes a back seat to the global.

As we move into the specific tools of Story Grid, we will keep coming back to this idea of our global/secondary and internal/external genres.

At this point, we've talked about genre (twice) and are getting a sense for the conventions and obligatory moments we need to identify for our story.

This gives us some language around the content of our story, but what is all this talk about the "value at stake"? We can see that Action is about life and death, but how does that apply in the on-the-ground writing of our story?

Now we have to talk about value shifts.

4
VALUE SHIFTS

When I began working with Shawn, he would often tell me that something has to happen in every scene. He said most beginning writers have scene after scene, sequence after sequence, where *nothing happens*.

I didn't fully understand this until I looked closely at some of my old writing.

Sure enough, I had scene after scene where nothing happened.

I think this is because of fear. When we're starting out writing, we don't really know what we're doing, so we write a lot of description and dialogue and character activity, but we avoid deciding what happens next.

It's like my dog that is afraid to come down the stairs.

He paces and whines and takes one step, then backs up and paces and whines, and takes another step, and finally after five minutes of movement but no progress, he does the thing he could have done from the beginning. He comes down the stairs.

The thing that helped me overcome this affliction was to think about value shifts.

When we say nothing happens in a scene, what we're really saying is there is no value shift. The character hasn't moved closer to or further from what they want or need. Something has happened in our scene only if we can point to a change on a spectrum of value that relates to our genre.

In an Action story scene, for instance, the value for our character must shift from life toward death or vice versa. If our character is safe at the beginning of the scene and still safe at the end of the scene, even if we wrote a couple of thousand words of conversation and action, *nothing happened.* We wrote about my dog pacing at the top of the stairs but never got to the part where he actually comes down the stairs.

Obviously, this doesn't mean a bomb has to go off in every scene. But it means the protagonist's situation has to move toward one side of the spectrum or the other—safe to unsafe (+ to -), love to hate (+ to -), ridiculed to popular (- to +), hope to despair (+ to -), confusion to clarity (- to +), peace to war (+ to -).

It also doesn't have to be an enormous shift.

Let's take that last one, for example—peace to war.

This can be a moment in our story when the dictator of the country declares war on the allied forces, or it can be that moment when your character's mother-in-law says *she* is making the Thanksgiving turkey this year.

We could describe either as a shift from peace to war (+ to -).

Think about how this adds another important tool to our toolbox. As we write our stories, we can be aware of value shifts. If we write a scene where nothing happens, that's something we can fix right away.

Also, when it comes time to work with our editor and she says something like, "I don't feel like this scene is going anywhere," we immediately realize it's time to identify a value shift in our scene. If we can't find the value shift, it's time for a rewrite. (Honestly, if our editor can't find the value shift, that probably means it's time for a rewrite.)

Our character has to be at one place on a value spectrum at the beginning and shift to either a more negative or more positive place by the end of the scene. If they don't, something is wrong. Nothing happened. It doesn't work.

Ok, so this is helpful. Every part of story has to have a value shift.

Next obvious question—how do we shift a value?

I can buy a new chest of drawers from Ikea and know at the end of the process I will have an assembled chest of drawers, but it's helpful to have a step-by-step process for how that is going to happen.

This is where the Five Commandments of Storytelling come into play, but before we can get to that, we have to talk about the parts of our story.

5

THE UNITS OF STORY

My younger son, Max, has always loved the building bricks from Lego. The problem is, they're a real pain in the ass to clean up. And when he was four or five, he would get really overwhelmed when it was time to clean up all the bricks strewn across the floor.

To help him, we took the enormous problem of cleaning up his floor full of bricks and created a handful of small piles that he could clean up one at a time.

It made a job that seemed insurmountable manageable by breaking it down into smaller pieces.

Up to now, we've been looking at our entire global story so we can figure out the values at stake, what the big conventions and moments in our story need to be, and how to shift them in the correct way.

But at the end of the day, we're still staring

down a 50,000, 100,000, or 200,000-word story we have to write.

That's too big for me to wrap my head around, especially as a beginning writer.

Instead, let's break this big problem into smaller problems that are easier to digest.

How do we do this? What are the smaller parts of the large story we can break it into?

The highest level is the whole start-to-finish story. That's our entire manuscript.

The next level down is our quadrants. The Beginning Hook, Middle Build 1, Middle Build 2, and Ending Payoff. That breaks our story down into four pieces that are roughly the same size.

This is where we can start applying some useful story math.

The Beginning Hook should be about 25 percent of our total word count. The Ending Payoff is another 25 percent. Then the Middle Build is 50 percent. Then we split the Middle Build into two equal parts—Middle Build 1 and Middle Build 2—that are each 25 percent.

So if we're thinking through a novel that will be 50,000 words, each quadrant of the story gets about 12,500 words.

How is this helpful?

First, as we're writing the novel, we can keep these numbers in mind. As we're approaching the 25 percent mark on our expected word count, we know we should be wrapping up the beginning of the story. Our protagonist should be entering the extraordinary world, and we should be starting Middle Build 1.

I recently finished the first draft of my next novel, and these markers were a huge help. They became points of reference on a really long journey. Writing without them would be like planning a road trip from New York City on the East Coast of the United States to Los Angeles on the West Coast without maps or GPS.

Instead of trying to drive the whole way in one shot and hope we make it there, we break the journey up into chunks. First, I have to get about a quarter of the way, to Pittsburgh, Pennsylvania. Then the halfway mark is about Omaha, Nebraska. Then, once I'm through Denver, Colorado, I know I'm almost there.

Looking at our novel, the first 25 percent (Beginning Hook) is where a problem arises related to basic human need and our protagonist (or luminary agent) reluctantly agrees to deal with it. Throughout the Middle Build 1 our luminary agent uses her best skills to solve the problem, but everything fails, and about 50 percent in, she falls into chaos. In Middle Build 2, the luminary figure tries to navigate the chaos and finds a novel way to approach the problem by the 75 percent mark. In the Ending Payoff, the last 25 percent, the luminary agent applies her new tools and skills to resolve the problem.

Can you see how breaking the whole story into smaller units helps you plan and draft your story?

It also helps on the editing side. When we evaluate our first draft, we can look at the four quadrants, and they should be roughly the same percentage of our story. If we look at our manuscript and we're approaching 35 percent of our word count and still setting up our story, *that could very well be a problem.*

I'm going to be honest here. When Shawn introduced me to this idea, I didn't buy it. It seemed too simple and, again, formulaic.

But then I started paying attention.

When I first read *11/22/63* by Stephen King, I was still early in my journey with Story Grid. When Jake Epping, the luminary agent of the story, transitioned into the extraordinary world, I stopped and checked how far I was through the book. It was 26 percent. When my wife and I watched *The Family Man* and the luminary agent, also named Jack, reached his point of no return and transitioned from Middle Build 1 to Middle Build 2, I paused the movie and, sure enough, we were halfway through!

Obviously, there are exceptions, but the vast majority of stories fit this form and, as a newbie writer, I've found, if it works for the great storytellers, I'm going to stick with it for now!

The next level down from the quadrant is the sequence. The sequence is a group of three to five scenes that move the story forward in a significant way. You could think of these as mini missions on the way to achieving the luminary agent's global mission.

The final level is the scene itself. Scenes usually average 1,500 words. Again, there is some variation here and there should be. If every scene we write is 1,500 words, the book won't feel right. However, when we're thinking through our novel, this rule of thumb can give us a rough sketch of how our story is going to look.

Let's assume we're writing a story, and we think it will be about 60,000 words.

If we break that down into quadrants, that comes to 15,000 words per quadrant. If we divide that by 1,500 words, it gives us ten scenes. If a sequence is three-to-five scenes long, then we are looking at about three sequences per quadrant.

Shawn introduces a smaller story unit, beats, inside of *The Story Grid*, but I believe in almost every instance it's not helpful to get down to a beat-by-beat investigation of our story, so we'll stop at the scene level.

Breaking our word count into quadrants, sequences, and then scenes gives us a useful starting point for our writing. We've taken our giant pile of Lego bricks and separated them into manageable piles.

I can't stress enough here that these are not crazy strict rules your story must follow. They're like staking out a house with sticks and string. We're getting a rough idea of how it should look before we pour concrete.

Once we are writing, it can be helpful to look at these different parts of our story to see if it is working—to see if there is a value shift.

How do we know if there is a value shift? Now we can dive into the Five Commandments of Story—our step-by-step guide to creating value shifts.

6

FIVE COMMANDMENTS

If I learned one bit of knowledge from Shawn that I use more than any other, it is this. If our value doesn't shift, we are breaking one (or more) of the Five Commandments of storytelling.

The Five Commandments are the step-by-step how-to methodology for creating value shifts in our story.

First, I'll give a quick introduction to the commandments and then dive into why they have been so helpful. I'll use the first scene of *Pride and Prejudice* by Jane Austen along with Shawn's explanation of the Five Commandments.

Inciting Incident. This is the unexpected event that kicks off the action in our story. These can be causal—a character actively does something—or coincidental—something random happens. Whatever it is, something has to get the story or scene going.

The inciting incident in the first scene of *Pride and Prejudice* happens when a bachelor—Mr. Bingley—rents a nearby manor.

Turning Point Progressive Complication. As the character(s) try to reach their goal of making the world right again after the inciting incident, they experience obstacles and sometimes tools along the way. These Progressive Complications build to a Turning Point that forces the character's hand. The character can no longer avoid confronting their problem, and this pushes them into the crisis.

In our *Pride and Prejudice* scene, Mrs. Bennet is trying to get Mr. Bennet to visit Mr. Bingley. She keeps giving him reasons to go, and he keeps batting these aside. Eventually, the real complication arises in that social convention requires the family must be formally introduced.

Crisis. The Crisis arises from the Turning Point Progressive Complication. The Crisis is a question. Will your character do X or Y? Will he fight or run? Will she rise to the occasion or allow herself to be subjugated? The Crisis is the point when your character has to decide.

In the first scene of *Pride and Prejudice*, the Crisis poses the question, will Mr. Bennet do what his wife is asking and visit Mr. Bingley or not be bothered with paternal duty so he can continue enjoying his private time?

Climax. The Climax is the answer to the question. It's when your character takes the action. When they choose, for example, *X* or "to fight" and act on that decision.

In *Pride and Prejudice*, Mr. Bennet refuses to visit the new bachelor. Even a choice to do nothing is a choice.

Resolution. This is what happens *as a result* of your character's decision.

As a result of their father's choice, the Bennet girls will remain without prospects.

Mrs. Bennet felt hopeful that her daughters could meet an eligible bachelor when she learned he has moved into the neighborhood, but she ends in despair because her husband refuses to go meet Mr. Bingley.

Here's another hypothetical example.

I wake up in the morning (Inciting Incident), which means it's time to make coffee.

I get up, gather the filter, measuring spoon, and Aeropress coffee maker. I put the Aeropress together, turn it over and realize I haven't ground any coffee yet. I hit the button to grind my coffee, but no grinding happens. Just the whirring of the blades. I'm out of coffee. I look for more coffee under the cabinets and in the pantry.

I come to the terrifying conclusion there is

no coffee (Turning Point Progressive Complication).

Now I must choose. Do I get dressed, go out in the below-freezing weather, start my car, drive to the grocery store, get more beans, and come home so I can have my coffee? Or do I suck it up and not have coffee this morning until I get to the office (Crisis)?

I put on my jacket, hat, and shoes, grab my keys, wallet and phone, and head out into the cold (Climax).

Thirty minutes later, I'm sitting on my couch drinking a fresh, hot cup of coffee (Resolution). Order is restored.

These Five Commandments work on every level of story. They apply to our global story along with every quadrant, sequence, and scene.

If we can't identify *all* Five Commandments in every unit of our story, *something is wrong.*

For instance, we could have four scenes that make up a sequence and each individual scene abides by the Five Commandments, but if the sequence doesn't go anywhere—if there is no shift—returning to my previous metaphor, it's merely a longer version of my dog pacing at the top of the stairs.

My dog *does* make progress when he steps down to the first step. If that was a scene, it would work. There was a value shift. He went from zero stairs to one stair.

But if the next scene reveals him backing up, and the following scene we see him pacing and whining, which is where we started our sequence, then even though the individual scenes work, our sequence doesn't as a whole.

In order for a story to be a story, something has to happen. When something happens in our story, that means we've abided by all Five Commandments. It's that simple.

Here's how I use these Five Commandments in practice.

When I'm planning my novel, I want to have a general idea of where I'm going but leave it loose enough that the story can take on a life of its own.

I start by identifying the Five Commandments in my entire story. I figure out what is going to kick off the action, what will force my protagonist into the final, big decision point, and then think out the Crisis, Climax, and Resolution.

Now that I have these global landmarks in place, I look at the next big section of my story I have to tackle. If I'm starting a new story, I look at the Beginning Hook—the first 25 percent of my novel. I think through the Five Commandments of that story unit knowing the Resolution will be my protagonist moving out of the ordinary world and into the extraordinary world.

Once that is done, I think through the Five Commandments of the next three to five scenes I have to write. Where is that sequence going? What is going to happen?

Finally, I'm down to the scene I'm about to write.

After practicing this for a few years now, I don't have to think through each of the Five Commandments consciously when I begin a scene, though that's how I started and practiced for a long time. Now it's more of a rough understanding that my scene is *going somewhere*. From the beginning of the scene to the end of the scene, a value must have shifted for my character.

The moment this came together for me I really fell in love with Story Grid. This idea that I can zoom out and evaluate my story at a macro level and then zoom in to an individual unit of my story and evaluate it on a micro level with the exact same set of questions astounded me.

7
POINT OF VIEW

I recently revisited my first nonfiction book, *Your First 1000 Copies*, and rewrote it from the ground up for the second edition.

With my experience, the rewrite should have been easy. But I kept having to start and restart the writing. I would draft a couple chapters, realize I was spinning off into directions I didn't want to go, and then have to back up and rework them.

What's crazy is I already knew exactly what I was trying to say in the book. It was the same basic material from the first edition with maybe 20 percent added or updated based on what I had learned in the seven years since it was first published.

Plus, I had already written this book before. Why was it so hard?

It came down to the point of view.

In the past, when I thought of point of view, I thought strictly of first-person, third-person, free indirect, omniscient, etc., but there is much more to it than that.

In fact, Story Grid Publishing has a book by Leslie Watts titled *Point of View* where she tackles this problem in depth.

The flowchart she presents includes these questions:

- Why are you writing this story?
- What is the best vantage point from which to present it?
- What narrative device should you choose?
- What is the effect of the narrative device?
- Which point of view choice best creates this effect?

In my rewrite of *Your First 1000 Copies*, I wanted to share what I know about book marketing with the reader. When I thought of the vantage point, I realized this was the sticking point for me in the way I was writing the book. I kept trying to write it as if I was the guru on the mountain doling out wisdom, but in reality, when I work with authors, it is always a collaborative process. Yes, I share my experience and expertise, but I do it in a partnership between the author and me.

I decided my vantage point shouldn't be the guru on the mountain. Rather I should come down and walk alongside the reader to have them discover how it works alongside me.

When we understand the vantage point, we can think about the narrative device that best mimics this situation. We can ask questions like these (also from *Point of View*):

- Who tells or shows the story?
- To whom?
- Where and when is the story being told or shown relative to the story events?
- In what form is the story being told or shown?
- Why?

I wanted to tell the reader about two of my clients I had worked with and walk them from start to finish through their book marketing process. The ultimate effect of this narrative device was exactly what I was going for. It allowed the reader to walk alongside the characters of my book and learn with them.

In my most recent novel, I picked third-person limited point of view. This allowed me to tell a story about my theme (more on that in the next chapter) from a vantage point where I could reveal what was happening in the story as if the reader were watching it with me. The narrative device is like an observer telling a story to the reader.

That sounded pretty good to me, but I'll be honest with you. Point of view is one of those subjects that continually evades my complete understanding. I often think I get it, but when it comes time to apply it to my writing, I quickly get lost.

When in doubt, we go back to the masterworks in our global genre. We grab our well-worn copies of books that inspire us and look at how those authors solve the same problems we have.

Harry Potter and the Sorcerer's Stone is written in third person limited with almost every scene presented from Harry's perspective. After the initial scene where Dumbledore drops Harry at the Dursley's, everything is seen from Harry's vantage point.

When I started writing what would become my first published novel, *The Threshing*, I reread the first *Harry Potter* novel and decided to follow this example. It felt easier to write in third-person limited and to tell the story from one person's perspective. And, if it works for J.K. Rowling, maybe it can work for me.

Our point of view drives everything in the story. We need to pick it carefully, and when in doubt, we copy a writer we admire who told a similar story to the one we are telling.

8

THEME

I put off writing this chapter until the very end. Theme is perhaps the slipperiest subject to discuss. It's like trying to grab ahold of a fish. Just when you think you understand it, it slips out of your grasp.

It helps me to remember that another phrase for theme we use inside of Story Grid is Controlling Idea. This central idea drives our story.

The first place we look to find our theme is the value at stake in our global genre.

If we're writing an Action story, we're talking about life and death. Love story deals with love and hate. Crime stories explore justice and injustice.

Our theme is something that we, as a writer, believe about the value shift and want to try and convey to the reader through our story. We identify this as the reason or cause driving the value shift from the beginning to the end of the story.

It can be deep and meaningful as in *The Great Gatsby*, a Worldview plot where the luminary agent moves from belief to disillusionment. We could say the theme of that story is "disillusionment comes when you believe money will buy love and fulfillment."

The theme can also be straightforward, such as *Casino Royale* and other James Bond novels where we could say the theme is "life conquers death when people are willing to sacrifice everything for the safety of their country."

I think of theme as answering the question: What do we want people to believe when they are done reading our story?

Our theme may change often as we work our way through our story. Most writers have trouble identifying their theme until the book is finished. In fact, many writers need their editor to tell them what the theme is once they've finished a manuscript.

It's just like the way we are not aware of our own internal scripts that drive our lives without us realizing what is going on.

However, once we have discovered and locked in the theme, we can go back and punch it up throughout our story.

If we're writing a Performance story, we

know it needs to turn on the value spectrum of respect to shame. We can look at all the different levels of our story and the obligatory moments to ensure they turn on these values.

But wait, if a story's theme focuses on the same values as all stories in the genre, does it mean the theme for Performance stories will all be the same?

No, there are lots of different levels and ways to interpret respect versus shame.

For example, these two different themes could drive a sports Performance story:

- We gain respect when we win, no matter what the cost.
- We gain respect when we play honorably and to the best of our ability, even if we lose.

We can see from these examples that even when the same value is at stake, we can express very different themes with our stories.

Once we have written a draft or two and identified our theme, we can review our story units and obligatory moments to ensure that not only do they turn on the correct value, but they also turn in a way that *reflects our theme*.

9

MACRO AND MICRO TOOLS

I use two tools inside the Story Grid Universe most often and incorporate the vocabulary we've discussed in this Story Grid Beat.

The first is the Story Grid Foolscap.

This is the macro view of our story.

It is the tool for putting our entire novel on a single sheet of paper.

You can see examples of a Foolscap at storygrid.com/story-language.

At the top of the Foolscap, we enter this information:

- Global genre and the value at stake
- Secondary genre (if we have one) and the value at stake
- Conventions and obligatory moments for our global genre
- Point of view

- Global and secondary Objects of Desire
- Controlling Idea/Theme

Then at the bottom of our Foolscap, we lay out each of the quadrants of our story, identifying the Five Commandments of each and noting whether they shift from negative to positive or positive to negative.

I think of the Foolscap as a way to check the vitals of my story. It's similar to how our visit to the doctor, no matter what it's for, includes a check of our pulse, blood pressure, and breathing.

I fill out a Foolscap for my story several times through the writing and editing process. I think of the Foolscap as a living document that we change as we write and edit. That's totally fine. The goal of the Foolscap is not to carve the details in stone from day one, predicting how our story will play out. The goal is first to make sure we understand what kind of story we are telling and second to ensure our story is moving in a direction and aligning with the genre.

The second of these two vital tools in our toolbox is the Story Grid Spreadsheet.

This is how we get a micro, scene-by-scene view of our story.

You can see examples of a Spreadsheet at storygrid.com/story-language.

For every scene of our story, we fill out the columns with our scenes' vitals that tell us if and how well they are working. In the basic Story Grid Spreadsheet, we fill out fourteen things for every scene:

- Scene number
- Word count—How many words are in the scene?
- Story event—a summary of what happens in the scene.
- Value shift—a description of the value that shifts in the scene.
- Polarity shift—Does the value shift from positive to negative or negative to positive?
- Turning point—At what point in our scene does the value shift?
- Point of view—From whose point of view is the scene presented?
- Period/Time—At what point in time does the scene take place?
- Duration—How much time passes during the scene?
- Location—Where does the scene take place?
- On-stage characters—Which characters are present in the scene?

- Number of on-stage characters—How many of them are there?
- Off-stage characters—Which characters are mentioned in the scene (but are not present and active)?
- Number of off-stage characters—How many of them are there?

Filling out a Story Grid Spreadsheet is its own deep subject, and the details are beyond the scope of this book. When you are ready to dive in and learn more, we have resources available at storygrid.com/story-language.

The goal of the Spreadsheet is to track, at the scene level, what is happening in the story. Several benefits flow from doing this work. First, it forces us to look at our scenes and decide if something has happened and, if so, what value shifted. We want to know if the value shift in the scene impacts our global and secondary genres.

When we are in the middle of writing our drafts, we often end up with scenes that don't shift, have an extremely weak shift, or shift in a way that doesn't affect the global or secondary values. These scenes may take us on a detour through exposition or unnecessary events. We can't see this when we simply reread our story. However, we notice these problems easily by dissecting the scene data into columns on the Spreadsheet.

The Spreadsheet also allows us to identify continuity problems. Do we have too many short scenes in a row? Are five scenes from one point of view and just one scene from another? Do the characters stay in the same location for too long? Are there time gaps in our story that don't make sense? Does a character or an important secondary character appear too infrequently?

Again, all of this is easy to miss when reading but impossible to miss when viewed through the lens of the Spreadsheet. The Spreadsheet forces us to see what's actually on the page as opposed to what we think is there. Often it's hard to see what our story has become because we're so close to it. However, as we like to say in the Story Grid Universe, you can't hide from the Spreadsheet.

The other thing I love about the Spreadsheet is its flexibility. You can add columns if you want to track different things. I always add a notes column so as I map out my story, I can add reminders of things I need to fix. This keeps me from getting bogged down trying to address problems while I'm filling out the Spreadsheet, which is an easy trap to fall into.

I'm going to be honest with you.

Completing the Spreadsheet is a painful process. I dread it every single time I have to do it, but I'm always glad once it's done. It is the single most important tool for finding problems in our story.

I'm currently working on the Spreadsheet for the first draft of my most recent novel. I'm only a dozen scenes in and have already identified several continuity problems and a scene with no coherent shift. I have a couple dozen notes of things I need to do in the second draft.

Once the spreadsheet is done, we have a view of our novel that is impossible to obtain any other way.

These two tools—the Foolscap and Spreadsheet—give us two important views of our story. Shawn is always recommending that we switch between the macro and micro view when working on our story. If we get stuck on the micro, we zoom out and look at the macro and vice versa. These tools allow us to do that.

When I'm stuck on what should happen with a scene and what value should shift, I step back and think about where the scene fits in the sequence, quadrant, or global story. I think about what comes before and after it in the Foolscap and which conventions or obligatory moments I could set up. If I'm struggling with the macro view of my story, I can zoom in and look at scenes and sequences to see if they're building in the correct way.

These two tools—the Foolscap and Spreadsheet—enable us to see our story clearly and identify if it is working on both the micro and macro levels.

10

HOW I USE STORY GRID TOOLS

My desire from the beginning was to offer tools you can use to create better stories and a common language to think about and discuss the use of those tools. This allows us to become better editors of our own work while also, when the time comes, making it easier to work with our editor.

In this final section, I want to walk you through a process I use to apply the tools in my own stories. Obviously, nothing is magical about the way I do it. Every writer who employs the Story Grid method can and should find the way that works best for them and their style. If you're just starting out, though, this is a good place to begin.

Whenever I'm starting a new writing project, there is a constant tension between the two "writers" who sit on my shoulders. One wants to plan my story meticulously before I write anything. Often called the Plotter in writer circles, this part of me is driven by fear. I don't want to waste time writing a story that never ends up going anywhere, so I try to plan everything from the start. The other part of me is free and confident. He's the Pantser of the pair and wants to take that seed of an idea for a story I woke up thinking about and start writing. He trusts the muse will show me the way.

Of course, they're both wrong.

I know from experience that trying to plan the perfect story down to the scene-by-scene detail before I begin writing is a fool's errand bound for frustration. Whatever plan I have will fall apart. Even if it did work, it would be devoid of the special things that arise from nowhere while we write. But I also know the Pantser is out of his mind. I'll start writing and generate tens of thousands of words that never actually go anywhere or coalesce into a story.

So I've made a deal with the two of them.

I promise the Pantser I will leave plenty of room for the muse in my work and won't plan too much. But I also lay out some guideposts in advance to keep my Plotter from freaking out.

Before writing the first word, I start with a Foolscap.

I decide on the global and secondary

genres. This allows me to know what values are at stake throughout the story.

Then, based on the genres, I make a list of all the conventions and obligatory moments my story must have, and I make a loose plan of how I will fulfill them all throughout my story.

Then I plan my point of view and make a rough draft of the theme.

Finally, I map out the Beginning Hook quadrant. If I feel like I have a good idea of what will happen in Middle Build 1, Middle Build 2, and the Ending Payoff, I'll fill those out too, but I don't worry too much about it.

I need to know how to begin, so I map out the Five Commandments of the Beginning Hook and get to work.

While writing my story, I never go back and fix things. I just keep writing forward. This is common advice from lots of prolific writers, and I agree with it.

I review my foolscap at different points in the process and update it with what I've learned of the story. When I finish one quadrant, I'll map out the Five Commandments of the next one.

The goal with these adjustments to the Foolscap is not to get it right. It's to keep my signposts ahead of me. I need to know what I'm writing toward.

. . .

As I start writing each day, I think about where I am in my sequence and quadrant and how that informs my current scene.

I keep up this process until a first draft is complete.

Once I've finished the first draft, I wade back into my Story Grid tools to review my work.

Keep in mind, Shawn Coyne developed the Story Grid methodology to help him as an editor. Obviously, the better we understand story, the better we're going to write our first drafts, but the Story Grid tools really shine when we apply them to editing our drafts.

The first thing I do is create a fresh Foolscap. If I kept my Foolscap up to date and referred to it as I was writing, this should be pretty straightforward. But I like to do it from scratch so I see everything with fresh eyes. I should be able to complete the entire top portion and also identify the Five Commandments of each of the quadrants.

The next thing I tackle is the Spreadsheet.

I go scene by scene through the entire story and fill out the columns in the Story Grid Spreadsheet.

This is tedious work and I recommend doing it a little bit at a time. I shoot for three to five scenes a day. I find if I do too many, I am tempted to rush through it.

I also keep a list of notes. I record anything that pops in my head that needs to be fixed in the second draft. Each note might be vague or specific. It can even be something as simple as "Figure out how the machine actually works." It's basically just a long list of to-dos that I will tackle in the next draft.

Once I'm done with this, I take a break from the story for a few days. This gives my brain time to work on everything after a lot of intense staring at the manuscript.

When I come back, I review my notes. This involves a lot of thinking and deciding. I often have a lot of world building to do and continuity issues to address as I think through my notes from the Spreadsheet in relation to the Foolscap.

The goal of the second draft is to have a story that works and is readable. As I write the first draft, I often change my mind and direction midstream. In the next draft, I apply those changes to the other parts of the book.

Once I've thought through everything and have made my decisions, I turn my notes into a to-do list.

This to-do list could include tasks as extensive as rewriting an entire sequence or as tiny as adding a single sentence to the fourth scene to set up what happens in the Ending Payoff.

The second draft is my favorite.

It's all about fixing problems. I feel confident I'm making the story better with every keystroke, but there's no pressure to make it perfect. In my mind, I'm shooting for about 80 percent done. It'll still require a lot of tweaking and tightening down, but someone could sit down and read the story start to finish, and it's not a train wreck.

Once the second draft is done, I recommend bringing someone else in.

At this point, we need someone with a fresh perspective—someone who can see the forest *and* the trees in our work.

My recommendation? Hire a Story Grid Certified Editor. We can hand them our Foolscap, Spreadsheet, and manuscript and have them immediately work through it with us because of the shared language and toolbox.

If we can't hire an editor, we can find another writer from the Story Grid Universe to work with. Again, this will allow us to use the common language outlined in this book and have useful conversations about how to make the story better.

My goal here is to have someone read the manuscript, review my Spreadsheet and Foolscap, and then come back to me with their own to-do list.

Once this is done, I review each scene and

look for ways to turn up the volume on the values at stake and continue weaving my theme into the manuscript.

The third draft should be written quickly. Unless our editor or friend found huge problems with our novel, it's a lot of making what we already have better.

When the third draft is complete, it's time to make some decisions. We can review the story a couple of more times with our editor to make it stronger, but it should be getting pretty close to finished.

From here, our goals for the story determine where we go next. Querying agents, submitting to a publishing house, or independently publishing are all on the table. What matters is we put in the work and applied the Story Grid tools to make the story the best we could at this point in our writing journey.

11

SHARED LANGUAGE AND TOOLBOX

When I finally read my copy of *The Story Grid* about six months after I purchased it, I realized I had stumbled upon something special. I couldn't put it into words at the time, but after working with Shawn for five and a half years, I've come to realize that what makes Story Grid so amazing is the shared language it brings to storytelling.

A word is only useful if we both mean the same thing when we use it.

The writing world is rife with words and phrases that mean different things to different people in different contexts.

By taking these words and grounding them with a common, high-resolution definition, we can think and talk about our story with clarity and specificity.

Now, when I talk about genre with another person who understands the Story Grid methodology, we both know we are talking about values at stake and the protagonist's primary need on Maslow's Hierarchy of Needs. If you had asked me about genre before Story Grid, I would have been all over the map talking about different things that have no real meaning.

The other thing Story Grid offers is a toolbox. The Foolscap and Spreadsheet are my favorite tools, but the Five Commandments, genre, and everything else we've discussed here are handy tools to pull out and apply to our story to make it better.

Once you can apply these tools to your own story, you will be amazed at the progress you can make in a short period of time.

12

BONUS: ANALYZING MASTERWORKS

What is the best way to train someone to spot counterfeit money?

When I first thought about this, I assumed you would need to study how the counterfeiters work and how they make the fakes. While this is part of it, the most efficient way to learn to spot counterfeits is to study the real thing.

Once someone becomes intimately familiar with the real thing, they can easily spot the fakes.

The same is true for writing.

How do we become a better writer?

Should we keep writing, repeating the same mistakes and hoping we get better through sheer brute force? Or should we learn from the masters?

This raises a question. How do we learn from the masters?

We hear stories of writers copying the masters word for word, typing entire published novels just to get the feel for how an author writes.

Which, I suppose, is our only option short of reading the novels and hoping they sink in through a sort of osmosis.

If we're studying a book this way, it's hard to know exactly what we're looking for. It's easy to get caught in the weeds of dialogue, characters, and prose—all the things on the surface.

The Story Grid methodology offers another way.

Using Story Grid, we have several tools that allow us to see a story in a new light.

First, we can identify the genre—the value that's at stake throughout the story. We can also observe how the storyteller employs the conventions and obligatory moments in their story.

We can dissect the story into quadrants, sequences, and scenes and look at these story units through the lens of the Five Commandments.

For example, my current work in progress is a global Action story and is the second book in a trilogy. So currently, I am analyzing the movie *The Empire Strikes Back* and entering what I find into the Story Grid Spreadsheet. Once I'm done, I'll review my work and fill out the Story Grid Foolscap. I did the same with *Harry Potter and the Sorcerer's Stone* and *The Hunger Games* when I was working on my first novel in the trilogy.

It's one thing to read these novels and try to understand how the author wrote these stories, but it's another to break them down using the Story Grid tools, which allow us to see them in a whole new light.

We don't want to use the Story Grid tools to look at our own stories only. Let's be honest, that's often like looking at counterfeits of real stories. We can use the tools to look closely at stories that have stood the test of time. This will help us level up our writing in ways we could never have dreamed.

ABOUT THE AUTHOR

TIM GRAHL is the author of *The Threshing, Running Down a Dream, Your First 1000 Copies,* and *Book Launch Blueprint.* For over a decade he has worked with top authors and creatives including Daniel H. Pink, Barbara Corcoran, Hugh MacLeod, Hugh Howey, Chip and Dan Heath, and many more. He now runs Story Grid Universe and Story Grid Publishing with his partner Shawn Coyne. See more of Tim's work at runningdownadream.com.

ABOUT THE EDITOR

LESLIE WATTS is a Story Grid Certified Editor, writer, and podcaster based in Austin, Texas. She's been writing for as long as she can remember—from her sixth-grade magazine about cats to writing practice while drafting opinions for an appellate court judge. Leslie has written craft-focused articles for the Fundamental Fridays blog and craft books, including *Point of View*, *Conventions and Obligatory Moments* (with Kimberly Kessler), *What's the Big Idea?* (with Shelley Sperry), and a masterwork analysis guide to Malcolm Gladwell's *The Tipping Point* (with Shelley Sperry). As an editor, Leslie helps fiction and nonfiction clients write epic stories that matter. She believes writers become better storytellers through study and practice, and editors owe a duty of care to help writers with specific and supportive guidance.

www.ingramcontent.com/pod-product-compliance
Lightning Source LLC
Chambersburg PA
CBHW071316080526
44587CB00018B/3249